wild and scenic
NEW ZEALAND

CRAIG POTTON

CRAIG
POTTON
PUBLISHING

INTRODUCTION

New Zealand is extraordinary for two reasons. Firstly, it is an isolated chunk of a once great Southern Ocean continent called Gondwanaland that split apart approximately 100 million years ago. When New Zealand separated from Australia it took a cargo of plants and animals that did not include that continent's newly emerging mammals and many families of flowering plants. Hence our plants and animals (especially birds like the kiwi) evolved in a series of eccentric sidestreams; they appear, quite correctly, to be ancient relics of time past. Our magnificent and once all pervasive forests can accurately be described as having felt the lost breath of dinosaurs.

Secondly, and here is where the beauty of the landscape marries the science of its creation, the landscape has been rucked about and contorted through our precarious position in the middle of a highly active junction of two huge continental plates. As a consequence the landscape has been torn apart by faults, mixed together by volcanoes, pressed together, thrust up and eroded down, subject to intense mountain-induced rainfall and semi-desert climes. In short, New Zealand's landscape has un-equalled contrast for a place of such small size: glaciers contend with volcanic and geothermal heat; semi-tropical beaches and forests merge with subantarctic oceans.

Laid over this intensely concentrated variety of natural wealth and beauty are the Maori and Pakeha cultures. Both arrived relatively late, Aotearoa/New Zealand being one of the last habitable places on earth to be colonised. The Maori bought their Polynesian tradition, the Pakeha were mostly English. Although both caused immense environmental damage, today, in a growing collective wisdom, we have achieved a high level of environmental protection of the remaining natural areas, and our cultures strive to respect the New Zealand landscape and its unique inhabitants.

A North Island brown kiwi noses through the undergrowth.

ABOVE: Lush sheep farms in the foothills of the Southern Alps near Fairlie, South Canterbury, where crisp, clear days such as this are a feature of winter.

TOP LEFT: Designed by English settlers far from home in the nineteenth century, Hagley Park in Christchurch is a haven of gardens, riverside walks and sports field.

BELOW LEFT: The former University of Canterbury buildings are now a centre for the arts, adjacent to the Canterbury Museum and the Robert MacDougall Art Gallery.

FAR LEFT: Cathedral Square with the iconic Christchurch Cathedral as its focal point, is another important city landmark. The imposing gothic buildings were designed by renowned architect Benjamin Mountfort.

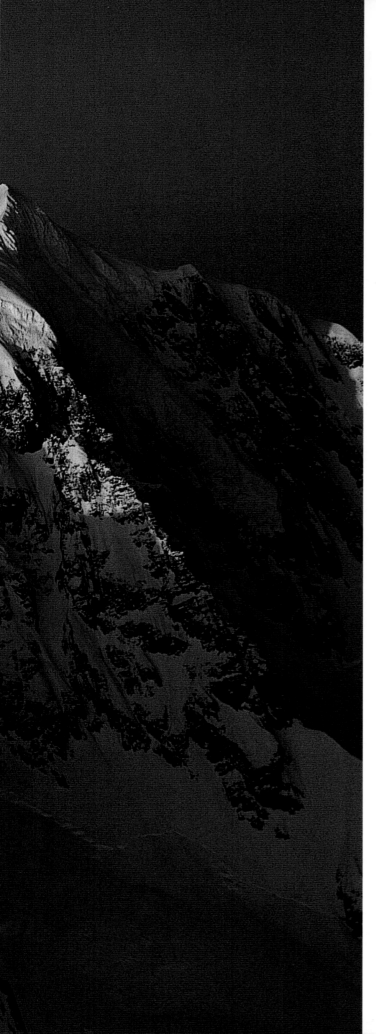

LEFT: The highest peaks of Aotearoa New Zealand are found in Aoraki/Mount Cook National Park. Seen here at first light are Aoraki/Mt Cook (left, 3754 m) and Mt Tasman (3498 m).

TOP: Moonrise over Mt Sefton, which towers over The Hermitage.

ABOVE: The world's largest buttercup *Ranunculus lyallii*.

ABOVE: The big empty skies over Canterbury's Mackenzie Basin will often fill with dramatic cloud formations, like these shower clouds building ahead of a front.

ABOVE RIGHT: A nor'west arch over Lake Pukaki, near Aoraki/Mount Cook National Park, portends bad weather.

LEFT: Lindis Pass, the southern gateway to the Mackenzie Basin from Otago, is a national reserve protecting an outstanding tussock grassland.

RIGHT: A winter storm carried by cold Antarctic southerlies leaves a deep blanket of snow over a cemetery near Burkes Pass.

ABOVE: Said to be the world's rarest penguins, yellow-eyed penguins nest on the Catlins coast in South Otago, an area rich in wildlife and forest.

FAR LEFT: Flowing 338 km across Central Otago from its source in the Alps to the east coast north of the Catlins, the Clutha River, pictured at Millers Flat, is the second longest in the country.

LEFT: 'Olveston', one of Dunedin's many fine historic buildings, is a 35-room Jacobean-style mansion in Dunedin, completed in 1906.

OVERLEAF: Lake Wanaka and Mt Aspiring.

TOP AND TOP RIGHT: You haven't been there and done that till you've jumped from one of Queenstown's many 'bungy' platforms, and scored your video and the t-shirt.

ABOVE: The sublime beauty of the mountains at the head of Lake Wakatipu.

RIGHT: As well as bungy jumping, Queenstown fun-seekers can raft the Shotover and Kawarau rivers, or ski, heli-ski, mountainbike, tramp, climb and parapente.

TOP: Queenstown is the premier all-year-round tourist destination in the South Island, located on the shore of Lake Wakatipu beneath the Remarkables Range.

ABOVE: An evening walk along the Queenstown waterfront brings its own rewards.

RIGHT: While Queenstown's renown is for adventure sports, an *Earnslaw* cruise is a more sedentary way to enjoy the mountain views.

ABOVE RIGHT: Arrowtown has preserved its historical character with many buildings dating back to the gold mining days of the nineteenth century.

LEFT: Knife-edge ridges, high mountains, slender fiords and dense forests characterise the wilderness qualities of Fiordland National Park – the largest in New Zealand and part of the Te Wahipounamu South-West New Zealand World Heritage Area. The most famous of Fiordland's deep, glacier-carved fiords is Milford Sound, seen here from the air looking west toward the Tasman.

ABOVE: While Fiordland's climate is notorious for the amount of rain that falls, calm clear days allow perfect reflections of Mitre Peak (1692 m), the park's most famous icon.

TOP RIGHT: When it does rain, waterfalls present some spectacular sights. Greatly swollen by rainfall, Bowen Falls, a 160 m cataract, thunders into Milford Sound.

BELOW RIGHT: North of Fiordland, climbers ascend Mt Aspiring (3027 m) above the Bonar Glacier in Mount Aspiring National Park.

ABOVE: Mt Christina in Fiordland's Darran Mountains, rises above montane beech forests on the Routeburn Track, another of New Zealand's 'Great Walks'.

ABOVE RIGHT: Ridge upon ridge of mountainous Fiordland wilderness, pictured here above the country through which the Milford Track passes.

LEFT: Lake Te Anau fills a trough gouged by an Ice Age glacier on Fiordland's eastern flank.

RIGHT: West Ruggedy Beach on Stewart Island is one of many remote sections of coast touched by the island's northwest tramping circuit.

TOP : Lake Mackenzie, on the Routeburn Track, in Fiordland National Park.

ABOVE: Beech forest fringes clear pools in the north branch of the Clinton River, on the Milford Track.

RIGHT: Giant Gate Falls is one of many picturesque waterfalls along the Milford Track.

ABOVE: The broad tributary snowfield at the head of Fox Glacier, in Westland National Park, is dominated by the sculpted peak of Mt Tasman (3497 m), second highest in New Zealand.

FAR LEFT: The snowfield feeds accumulated glacier ice into the Fox Glacier, which plunges through a steep icefall towards coastal plains less than 300 m above sea level.

LEFT: North of the Fox lies the heavily crevassed Franz Josef Glacier, named in 1865 by the explorer Julius von Haast. Both glaciers are amongst the fastest flowing in the world, at between 3–4 metres a day. Heavy snowfalls through the 1980s and 1990s resulted in significant advances down valley by both glaciers.

TOP: Lowland beech forest interior south of Haast. Forests such as these have immense ecological value because lowland forests in the rest of New Zealand were decimated by logging.

ABOVE: All but the last two percent of kahikatea swamp forests, like this one on the shores of Lake Wahapo, have been wiped out – their greatest stronghold lies in this corner of South Westland.

RIGHT: The crescent sweep of Ohinemaka Beach, north of Haast, is fringed by coastal forest and wetlands.

ABOVE AND TOP: Tranquil days in South Westland are perfect occasions to visit Lake Matheson, a few kilometres west of Fox Glacier village, for early morning and late evening reflections of the highest peaks of the Southern Alps.

LEFT: Sheep graze grasslands on the coastal plains near Fox Glacier village below Mt Tasman.

ABOVE AND TOP: Lake Mapourika is one of a series of South Westland lakes formed at the end of the last ice age. Glaciers repeatedly advanced and retreated across the coastal plains during the ice age (between 70,000 and 14,000 years ago) and their final retreat left distinctive landforms including the beautiful lakes for which the area is renowned.

LEFT: Mt Tasman's west face looms over deep crevasses on the Fox Glacier.

LEFT: Paparoa National Park's most famous icon is the Pancake Rocks at Punakaiki, where spectacular geyser-like blowholes are particularly impressive in a strong westerly swell.

ABOVE: The dramatic North Westland coastline was all but inaccessible until the Westport–Greymouth road was completed in 1929. Nowadays tourists can gain access to the coast via bays and short walks that begin at Punakaiki.

TOP : The Truman Track is an easy walk through subtropical coastal forest, emerging at a wild coast with cliffs, caverns, blowholes and a waterfall.

TOP: The Porarari River in Paparoa National Park flows through a distinctive limestone canyon filled with lush mixed podocarp beech forest.

LEFT: One of several impressive limestone arches on the Oparara river, near Karamea in Kahurangi National Park. The arches are the result of millions of years of gradual dissolution of limestone by water.

ABOVE: The nikau is New Zealand's only palm, and the southernmost palm in the world. This stand is growing near Punakaiki where the unique geography has created optimum growing conditions.

LEFT: A guide on the lower reaches of the Fox Glacier in Westland National Park.

ABOVE: The Heaphy Track in Kahurangi National Park crosses the Gouland Downs, one of the high altitude tussock covered tablelands that are characteristic of the park's interior.

TOP: Trampers on the Heaphy Track cross dramatic stretches of West Coast beach with rolling surf, such as Scotts Beach pictured here.

OVERLEAF: A tramper on the jetty at the head of Lake Rotoroa in Nelson Lakes National Park. (Photo: Shaun Barnett/Black Robin Photography)

TOP: This aerial view of Abel Tasman National Park shows the indented sequence of bays and headlands that have made this one of New Zealand's most popular National Parks.

LEFT: Sunrise over Torrent Bay with The Anchorage on the left and the perfect horseshoe crescent of Te Pukatea Bay in the foreground.

RIGHT: The famous golden sands of the Abel Tasman coastline, rippled by the retreating tide and strewn with shells at Awaroa inlet.

TOP: A cloudy sunset over Haulashore Island and The Cut, leading into Nelson harbour.

ABOVE: Sunset over Tasman Bay and the Tasman Mountains, with Fifeshire Rock standing at the old entrance to Nelson harbour.

ABOVE RIGHT: Tussock flats in the Cobb Valley, with the heavily forested ranges of Kahurangi National Park behind.

RIGHT: The spectacular west coast of Golden Bay stretching south from Farewell Spit.

ABOVE LEFT: An aerial view of the Marlborough Sounds, looking over outer Pelorus Sound and the western end of Cook Strait.

LEFT: Pinot Noir grapes ripen in a Marlborough vineyard. Nearly half of New Zealand's Pinot Noir is planted in the region.

ABOVE: A sperm whale sounds off the coast of Kaikoura. Whale watching has become a major drawcard in Kaikoura, transforming what was a small fishing community into a thriving tourist centre.

RIGHT: Sheep graze on the Kaikoura Peninsula, indicating a more traditional way of making a living in this area.

ABOVE: New Zealand's capital city Wellington and the inner harbour. The harbour was originally part of the Hutt River, which feeds into it, but regular earthquake activity resulted in the land sinking and the area being submerged.

LEFT: Downtown Wellington at night, photographed from Mt Victoria.

PREVIOUS PAGE: A vineyard on the Wairau Plains near Blenheim, Marlborough. The particular mix of soil and climate in Marlborough has supported the spectacular growth of the of the wine industry here, led initially by the now world famous Sauvignon Blancs, but diversifying more recently into other varieties, especially Pinot Noir and sparkling wine.

TOP: Te Papa Tongarewa – The Museum of New Zealand, on Wellington's waterfront.

TOP RIGHT: Wellington's Civic Square features a suspended sculpture by Christchurch artist Neil Dawson.

ABOVE: The arched entrance of Napier's Rothmans Building, designed by Louis Hay in 1933. When Napier was destroyed by a massive earthquake, much of the city was rebuilt in Art Deco style.

RIGHT: Kapiti Island, north of Wellington, is an important wildlife sanctuary, home to many endangered species of birds.

OVERLEAF: In September 1996 Mt Ruapehu erupted for the first time in years, spreading ash over large parts of the North Island.

LEFT: The elegant cone of Mt Tongariro (1968 m) in Tongariro National Park. In Maori tradition, all three volcanic peaks in the park – Ruapehu, Tongariro and Ngauruhoe – are part of the one mountain complex of Tongariro.

TOP: Fishing for trout at Waitahanui on the shores of Lake Taupo, the largest lake in New Zealand. Taupo's rainbow trout, averaging around 2kg, are probably the only pure strain in the world.

ABOVE: A small fern-lined gorge in Whirinaki Forest Park in the Central North Island.

ABOVE: Bubbling mud pools near Rotorua are a sign of the geothermal activity taking place just below the surface of the earth in this region.

FAR RIGHT: Whakarewarewa is the best known of Rotorua's thermal areas, with the largest geyser, Pohutu, playing to a height of over 30 metres.

RIGHT: In addition to the natural environment, tourists are attracted to the cultural performances and Art Festivals which reflect the strong Maori heritage in the Central North Island. This poi dancer's tribe is Tuwharetoa.

LEFT: Beech forest on Panekiri Bluff above Lake Waikaremoana, the heart of Te Urewera National Park. Te Urewera is the homeland of the Tuhoe people, providing them with a place of refuge, healing and growth.

ABOVE: A carving from the marae at Whakarewarewa village, near Rotorua.

ABOVE LEFT: Two cavers abseil into the spectacular entrance to the Lost World Cave near Waitomo, in the King Country. The Waitomo caves are noted for their stalagmite and stalactite formations, and an extensive network of glowworm grottos.

LEFT: Horse riders on the beach at Tolaga Bay, on the remote East Cape of the North Island.

ABOVE: The Huka Falls are created where the powerful Waikato River, which has its source at Lake Taupo, is forced through a narrow gorge. The name Huka means "Foam".

RIGHT: An early winter snowfall catches the summit of Taranaki/Mt Egmont, the extinct volcano that defines the Taranaki region on the West Coast of the North Island.

LEFT: The Sky Tower, which opened in 1997, dominates the central Auckland skyline.

TOP: The Auckland War Memorial Museum houses the largest collection of Maori artefacts and carvings in the world.

ABOVE: Auckland's landscape is dotted with volcanic cones and craters. Rangitoto Island in the Hauraki Gulf was created during one of the more recent periods of volcanic activity, approximately 600 years ago.

ABOVE: Tane Mahuta, growing in the Waipoua sanctuary, is New Zealand's largest living kauri tree, with an estimated age of between 1200 and 1500 years, and a girth of 13.77 metres.

RIGHT: The massive bases of two kauri trees in Trounson Reserve. Kauri trunks grow straight and clean, and were prized as timber by both Maori and Europeans, leading to the destruction of the once extensive forests. The scattered remnants are now protected.

PREVIOUS PAGE: Auckland is known as "The City of Sails" from its location between Manukau and Waitemata harbours – in this shot the Sky Tower and downtown buildings form a backdrop to Westhaven Marina.

ABOVE: The extensive sand dunes of Ninety Mile Beach on Northland's west coast. The ocean beach is in fact only about 60 miles long, but it is an important source of the shellfish toheroa, and a haven for migratory birds.

LEFT: Motuarohia Island's sheltered waters, white sandy beaches and recreation reserve are typical of the many attractions which make the Bay of Islands a popular holiday destination.

RIGHT: Bringing ashore the morning catch of hapuku at Hicks Bay, on the East Cape north of Gisborne. The area is noted for its excellent fishing.

LEFT: Cape Reinga, at the north-west extremity of New Zealand, stands above the meeting point of the Tasman Sea and the Pacific Ocean. The name means "Place of leaping", because in Maori tradition it is where the souls of the departed leave for their future destination.

ABOVE: A full moon rises over the tranquil ocean.

Photographs: Craig Potton
Printed and bound by Astra Print Ltd,
Wellington, New Zealand

Published by Craig Potton Publishing,
98 Vickerman Street,
PO Box 555, Nelson, New Zealand

© 2000 Craig Potton Publishing
Reprinted in 2003

ISBN 0 908802 66 8

Front Cover: The podocarp forests of Waikukupa, Westland National Park, with Mt Tasman and Aoraki/Mt Cook behind.
Back Cover: Top: A small gorge in the Whirinaki forest, Central North Island.
Bottom: Maori carving, Whakarewarewa, Rotorua